Jacquie Murrell

LIFE SUPPORT
Surviving Life's Worse Challenges

Literacy

© Copyright 2015 **Jacquie Murrell**

LIFE SUPPORT

Published by Literacy in Motion
PO BOX 11892 Merrillville IN 46411-1892

Anthony KaDarrell Thigpen editorial services, a subsidiary of Literacy in Motion.

Library of Congress Cataloging-in-Publication Data Published and Printed by Literacy in Motion

Cover Design by Literacy in Motion Design Team
LIFE SUPPORT
ISBN: 978-0-9904440-5-3

Graphics and Editing by Anthony KaDarrell Thigpen,
Editor in Chief

Self-Help and Religious Printed in the United States of America

Jacquie Murrell

DEDICATION

To my mother and father who birthed me into this world and did their best to take care of me. To every man, woman and teenager who feel like their pain, hurt, suffering and brokenness are beyond repair. If you feel like you have every reason to give up, throw in the towel and die; know that there is nothing in this world that God cannot do. Earth has no sorrow or pain that heaven cannot feel or heal.

Live by the "I AM" factor; always knowing, trusting and believing that you are everything God says you are and were called to be by allowing your faith to cancel the synthetic fear created by the seemingly big obstacles the enemy tries to destroy you with. The enemy is overpowered and conquered by an even bigger God who is the source of your every need. You must face "it" in order for Him to fix "it."

To my grandmother, Pastor David W. Greene Sr.. Aunt Paulette Holmes, cousin Vernita Hunter, godmother Tanya Northcross, friends; Stacey Taylor and Ashley Qualls; thank you for loving me, taking me in, pushing me and encouraging me through every single obstacle, mistake, and lesson to help me live a life without limits.

Life Support

CONTENTS

PREFACE

Humble yourselves, therefore, under God's mighty hand, that he may lift you up in due time. Cast all your anxiety on him because he cares for you. Be self-controlled and alert. Your enemy the devil prowls around like a roaring lion looking for someone to devour. Resist him, standing firm in the faith, because you know that your brothers throughout the world are undergoing the same kind of sufferings. And the God of all grace, who called you to his eternal glory in Christ, after you have suffered a little while, will himself restore you and make you strong, firm and steadfast. To him be the power forever and ever. Amen.

- 1 Peter 5:6-11

This book is the first of a 3-part series designed to be a motivational and teaching guide on how to recognize the issues, identify the root of the issues and implement a plan to rebuild yourself and your life.

Please understand that my transparency in this debut book is to enlighten, encourage and empower individuals and families that are experiencing obstacles that seem too big to overcome. I will share some very intimate details that most can identify with. This book covers the root of my previous issues and tells the story about how I faced some of life's greatest struggles and overcame them all. I survived abandonment, molestation, rape, homelessness, divorce, abortion, losing everything, and more; I had every reason to die, but because of my undying spirit I

I never gave up. I always knew that God had something great in store for me. This book is an account of how I went from a critical condition to the road to recovery. The second book in this series is "REHAB," as it gives you some insight to how I began rebuilding my life and giving readers practical tips on how to form and implement a plan to overcome all obstacles. It is also a living testament to how God is able to take a total disaster and begin turning it into total victory!

It was only through hard work, determination and by faith, grace, and mercy that I am an overcomer. Now I am able to walk in victory. God can do the same thing for you. He will fulfill His promise to you and complete the work that He started in you.

Chapter 1
BIRTHED INTO THE WORLD

We all are born into this world not knowing what we will encounter. Though we all are subject to different circumstances and hereditary characteristics, we ultimately make the choice to conform, become products of our environment or influence the environment to change.

I was born on June 25, 1983 in Indianapolis, IN. My mother had me at the age of 19 and married my father after I was born. I am the eldest child of three. My siblings and I are all a year apart from each other. We were inseparable. I had a fairly good childhood. We had fun and we shared everything. We had hardships and trying times along the way, but just like any other family we had our secrets too.

Though I had fun, love and laughter in the home I grew up in as a child, at times it could be very chaotic and scary. My mother and father use to fight and scream at each other all the time. There was a lot of domestic violence, drugs and alcohol in the home. I remember my father showing my sisters and I how to prepare and cook crack, as well as how to roll a joint which they called refer back then. I was about 4-years-old at the time. My parents were not ashamed of their lifestyle and didn't go to great lengths to hide it.

My mother was a singer in a band and a secretary. My father was a carpenter. My parents did make good money and we had everything we needed, even a nice car. My mother always kept me and my sisters groomed and dressed well from head to toe. I watched my parents so closely that when they would go out, I would pretend to do what they did. As a child, I remember my siblings and I knotting our shirts so that our stomachs would show, filling clear plastic cups with apple juice pretending it was liquor and using white candy sticks or crayons to pretend we were smoking. Now that I look back on it, I see what people mean when they say children do as you do and not as you say. We didn't realize at the time how much of an impression those things had on us and I don't think my parents realized it either.

I don't really remember the day my mother left my father as I was still very young, but I do know that my mother had enough of all the drugs, alcohol and fighting and my father didn't want to give it up as the drugs had a strong hold on him. I think my mother realized one day that it wasn't the kind of life she wanted for my sisters and I. My mother and father began raising me in the church and I think my mother started applying some of the things the minister was preaching about to her life and realized that God had better for her. So, my mother packed us up and we left.

THE ABSENCE OF A FATHER

It was hard on my mother raising three girls by herself. When she left my father, we attended church more often and she began to create a sense of order. I guess my father felt like he could be a part-time father since we didn't live in the same house as him anymore, which made it hard on my sisters and I as well.

My mother started working two jobs to take care of my sisters and I. Years passed and the visits with my father became less frequent. After that, I never saw my father unless I just happened to run into him in public. I knew who he was but because I was so young when my mother left him, I never got to know him and really form a relationship, but I knew I loved him. He became a distant memory that resurfaced every now and again.

Meanwhile, my mother had a few boyfriends and one of them even lived with us for a couple of years and none of them really took on the role of a father. I was heartbroken, angry, and disappointed. I felt like my father had abandoned me. I began to question myself as to whether or not something was wrong with me and ask why he never wanted to spend time with me. I knew my father was still a drug addict but as a child, I didn't understand that he was battling his own demons, which caused him to be less than what a father should be. By this time, I was about 8 or 9-years-old.

REMEMBERING GOD'S FIRST APPEARANCE

How many know that in the midst of every trial, hurt and sorrow; God is present? You may not recognize Him while you are in it and that may be because of young age or a disconnection between you and Him, but when He has a plan for your life, He will be there through it all to make sure He finishes what He began in you?

In light of the changes that I was going through and some of the things I had seen, I was still fortunate enough to be favored among my grandparents though during the years of my childhood, they had 40 plus grandchildren. My grandmother was and still is like a second mother to me. My grandfather was my daddy. I love them dearly. I spent an enormous amount of time at my grandparents' house and at one point I was even going to school from there. I would spend the summers there as well. It was such a different atmosphere than the one at home. Even though my mother raised me in church, I would go to church with my grandparents as well while I was with them. I never witnessed an argument or a fight until I was a pre-teen and even then it was only once. There wasn't anything my grandparents wouldn't do for me. You could say it was a little piece of heaven for me.

They taught me a lot of things growing up. The home atmosphere was peaceful. My grandparents are God-fearing people. There wasn't a day that went by that I didn't see my grandmother getting down on her knees to pray before she went to bed and getting down to pray as soon as she woke up in the morning. Also, there wasn't a day she didn't take time out to read her bible. Sometimes she would read it to me and when I got old enough, I would read with her and she would explain what we read and answer my questions. Little did I know they were depositing good seeds into me.

I had a fairly good and fun childhood in spite of some of the things I saw, was taught, and experienced. Now that I look back, I realize God was present through my grandparents during my childhood years.

CHAPTER 1, SELF-REFLECTION

The first step after admitting you have unresolved issues is to identify the root (underlying factors) of those issues. You must face them in order to begin healing in every area that you are hurt. You may be a part of a generational curse. Whether you were born into chaos or are a part of a generational curse, God is able to break every chain, but it must start with you. As long as you have the same mindset and harbor the same fears, hurt, habits and hang-ups, you cannot experience total liberation. I started out in life with only a few odds against me but God made sure there were good seeds sown in me so that I would be able to fulfill my purpose even in light of what He knew I would encounter. He was there in the beginning.

1.   Can you recall your beginning? If so, was there anything that you feel contributed to your previous and/or current learned behavior?

_____

_____

_____

2.   As you reflect back, can you identify where God was in your beginning? You may not have recognized Him then, but as you look back, do you see where He was present?

_____

_____

_____

Study Scriptures
Ephesians 2:10
Jeremiah 29:11

Chapter 2
SATAN'S PREMEDITATED MURDER PLOT

he enemy can see what God has placed in you and if it looks like it will be a threat in his plot to destroy you, he will do everything in his power to try and make sure you never fulfill your purpose and obtain everything God has for you. He does a very good job at tricking you into believing the opposite of what God has spoken over you before you were even formed in the womb. If he can separate you from God, he has the upper hand at winning the battle. He uses many different people, including those close to you as well as different circumstances to try and kill you mentally, emotionally, spiritually, and ultimately physically.

I was about 11-years-old when my mother decided that she was going to become a Muslim. I couldn't believe it! She was raised as a Christian and so was I. She insisted I follow the rules of the Muslims and live their lifestyle. I didn't want to be a Muslim. I felt like if that's what she wanted to do then that was fine but I wasn't going to live the lifestyle of a Muslim. I couldn't celebrate holidays anymore, I had to dress a certain way and I couldn't eat some of the things I had eaten all my life.

Though I was an honor roll student in school, I used to leave out for school in one outfit and then change when I arrived. My mother felt like I was being disrespectful. I was taught that no one could go to heaven or hell for you. I was taught that there is only one God and that He is a jealous God. I felt like disobeying God was worse than disobeying my mother when it came to religion. This put even more strain on the thoughts I was already having as a child dealing with so much mentally.

Eventually I just went along with it, but I never let it stick to me. I always knew in my heart that Jesus was real and that I would never believe otherwise or worship any other gods. I just didn't know how to utilize Him for what was beginning to fester within me.

My mother still went to church from time to time to sing or to see an old friend and every time she would enter the choir stand and begin to open her mouth to sing, I could just see this tremendous light in her. Every time she sang, she sang with everything in her as if she knew she still belonged there. I couldn't understand why she would try to make me accept anything other than Christianity when you could see her deeply rooted connection as she sang and it would just overtake her. That was His gift to her. She could move your soul.

Growing up around drugs and alcohol, arguing and fighting, absence of a father and being forced to believe in a faith other than Christianity was beginning to take a toll on me emotionally and mentally. I was very good at hiding it, but the wounds would soon begin to surface. The slow murder had begun at the moment my belief in Jesus was being pried from my life. If I was not taught anything else during my childhood, I was taught He was the ultimate lifeline. I was not old enough to understand what it meant to have a relationship with Him or how important it was to have one, but He was deeply rooted within and I refused to let go.

THE FIRST STAB WOUND

Once he completed the task of presenting a different faith and teaching in an effort to disconnect my lifeline to Jesus, the sharp stab wounds began. When I was 11-years-old, I stayed the night at a friend's house who happened to be my best friend at that time. We slept over at each other's house often, but this particular time was different as it would be the beginning of the enemy thickening his plot to murder me.

While staying over this particular weekend, my friend's mother (who we will call Ms. Smith) invited some friends over. They were talking and playing cards while my friend and I along with her 2 brothers were watching television. It was late so we were all in our pajamas. I was wearing a red thick cotton, long sleeved, ankle length nightgown with a pocket across the chest area. After some time had passed, Ms. Smith's friends left except for one and this particular friend brought another friend. They were both men. Ms. Smith, her daughter, the two men, the oldest brother (who we will call Joe) and myself began playing "Go Fish." The youngest brother fell asleep and got up to lie down in his room. Ms. Smith's friend said he had to leave for a little while and he would be back. He left the friend he invited with us. The man reeked of alcohol and we could tell that he was extremely drunk. He looked to be about 30 to 37-years-old. He was a light skinned man, about 5'7" with curly dark hair and a trimmed beard. I will never forget the way he looked.

As we continued to play cards, we struck up a conversation and the man told us that he had a daughter and showed us a picture. He also said that he had just got out of jail but he never told us what he was in jail for. Ms. Smith and her daughter began to get sleepy so we all stopped playing cards. Ms. Smith and her daughter stretched out on the couches and watched television until they fell asleep. Joe and I sat on the floor and watched television. The stranger sat across the room on the floor and watched television with us.

Joe nudged me and told me to look over to my left. The stranger was staring at me. It made me feel uneasy and a little scared. Joe and I knew something wasn't right about him. Joe told the stranger to call his friend to come and get him because he wanted to lock up the house. The stranger said he didn't know how to contact his friend and that he would just wait until his friend returned. It was about two o'clock in the morning.

A few minutes later, the stranger began to whisper to me saying, "Come here." I looked at the stranger and told him "no" and then turned back to look at the television. I was very afraid now. Joe told the man to leave me alone but he just kept on whispering to me. Joe was about 8 or 9-years-old and like I said before, I was 11-years-old, so the stranger really wasn't listening to us. Joe and I looked over at the couches at Ms. Smith and his sister. The stranger knew that we were thinking about waking them. The stranger told us to be quiet in a firm tone. We became overcome with fear. Joe and I were no longer sleepy. Now we were wide awake because we knew the stranger was drunk, had just gotten out of jail, and was up to no good.

I continued to ignore the stranger whispering to me. About five minutes later, the stranger slid across the floor, grabbed me by my arm and pulled me over to where he was sitting. I was instantly consumed with even more fear. I began to tremble. Joe told the stranger to leave me alone. The stranger told Joe to be quiet and said, "I'm not going to hurt her." The stranger was sitting on the floor with his legs straddled and he pulled me close to him so that my back was lying against his stomach. He wrapped his arms around me and I began to tremble all over as tears began to run down my face. I didn't utter a sound. I was so scared that I couldn't say anything. I was frozen with fear. I had never been so scared before. I thought if I screamed, he would hurt Joe or me. He whispered in my ear and asked me, "Why are you shaking?" He said, "I'm not going to hurt you." "Stop Shaking", he said.

Joe sat very still in front of the television. He looked like he was thinking of what to do to help me. In my mind, I wished that he would hurry up and think of something. Finally, I unfroze and tried to get loose from the stranger's grip while still crying but he just pulled me closer and wrapped his arms around me tighter. I just knew he was going to hurt me. He kept his left arm around my left shoulder and wrapped it around so that his arm stretched across the base of my neck and his hand rested on the right side of my neck. He began to slide his right hand down inside the top of my nightgown and began to fondle me by rubbing his hand across my breasts. I was frozen again, tears flowing. It felt like I was trembling so much that you would think I was having a seizure. Joe looked over and saw what the stranger was doing to me, and his face turned angry. He went into deep thought. I imagine he was thinking about how to save me. The stranger continued to fondle my breasts and tears continued to pour down my face and I still didn't utter a word. The stranger took his hand out of my nightgown and began to stroke my stomach. I began to shake uncontrollably. I just knew what he was going to do next. He placed his left hand around my waist and held me still. He took his right hand and placed it on my vaginal area. I don't know what happened, but something in me couldn't let him go further. Joe looked at me and knew I was about to do something. I was still very afraid but I had to try and escape again before my innocence was ripped from my body.

I jumped up and the stranger grabbed my arm and asked, "What are you doing?" "Where are you going?" he asked. I thought of something quick and said, "I'm going to the restroom." I ran to the restroom and Joe ran to his room. I tried to lock the door but there was no lock on it. I was pacing back and forth thinking about what to do next. I was crying and shaking. I heard someone coming down the hall. I backed up against the bathroom wall. The door opened and it was the stranger. He asked me what I was doing in the bathroom. I ran out past him and into my friend's room. Ms. Smith and her daughter were still asleep. Ms. Smith had been drinking so I knew she wouldn't wake even if we tried to shake her. They couldn't hear anything because Joe and I were quiet like the man told us to be because we thought he would definitely hurt us. Our need to get rid of him was stronger than our fear now.

My friend's room was pitch black. I thought I could hide in there. She didn't have enough space under the bed for me to crawl under it. The closet had too much stuff in it for me to fit in there so I laid down flat in her bed and pulled the covers over my face. I prayed he didn't see where I went. He was drunk so he was moving kind of slow and staggering. I heard a noise in the next room. It was Joe. He was in his room looking for something.

Even though my mother had become a Muslim and was forcing me to adapt to that lifestyle, it was only surface deep. While I lay in the pitch black room under the covers, I remembered my grandma praying and teaching me how to pray to ask God for whatever I needed. I was still so scared. I was still crying and shaking and tried to stay quiet so the stranger wouldn't find me. I began to pray. I said, "God please don't let this man find me and get me."

I heard the door open slowly. I peeked out from the side of the covers. It was the stranger. As I pulled the cover back up over my eyes, I heard the door close. I thought he left. I looked out from under the cover and he was standing in the room. It was still dark. He began taking off his shoes and his clothes by the door. I sat so still in the bed paralyzed in fear. I thought if I got up to run again, he would stop me because he was right by the door. So I waited. He undressed down to his boxers and walked around to the other side of the bed and he got in the bed and lay down next to me. He tried to put his arm around me and I jumped up and darted out of the room back into the living room. Joe was waiting with his softball bat. He stood guard at the end of the hallway while I tried to wake my friend and Ms. Smith. I tried to wake them quickly and quietly so the stranger wouldn't hear us. I began to shake my friend to wake her. I was crying and frantic. I was begging her to get up. Joe told me to hurry. The stranger was coming out of the room but he was half dressed. My friend jumped up and asked what was wrong. I was trying to tell what had happened to me quickly and telling her that we should wake her mom. Joe was trying to tell her too. The stranger walked into the living room with his boots in his hand, his pants half pulled up and he was just pulling down his shirt from over his head. My friend couldn't believe it! She yelled at him and said, "You got to get out!" It woke Ms. Smith and she was cursing at the stranger and pushing him out the door.

It was about four o'clock in the morning and Joe and I began to tell Ms. Smith and her daughter what happened. I couldn't stop crying and shaking. My friend was hugging me and Ms. Smith began to cry and tell me how sorry she was. Ms. Smith called the police and my mother.

The police arrived right before my mother did. My mother brought one of the men from the mosque with her. The police and the man from the mosque were asking me questions to make a report. We gave a description to the police. It had only been 15 minutes since the stranger left and he was on foot and staggering so the police figured he couldn't have gone far. After the police left, Ms. Smith was still crying and she was apologizing to my mother, telling her how sorry she was. My mother and the man from the mosque told me I should have called them. They were talking to me like they were angry with me. Their tone was as if it was my fault. In my mind, it was like they were saying that I could have prevented it. I felt so helpless, alone and like it was my entire fault. That is large burden for an 11 year old to bear. They made me feel worse than I had already felt but I never expressed it. To make matters worse, the stranger was never found.

From that day forward, I didn't really trust anyone and I felt like I couldn't trust my mother either. I made up in my mind that I would just hold everything in and deal with it. I would keep everything to myself. I felt like I couldn't talk to her. We never told anyone else what had happened that night. We never talked about it again. I never got a chance to vent or to heal from it. It was just swept under the rug. I wasn't allowed to go over my friend's house anymore. We started talking less and less to each other. As time went by, we lost contact with each other.

I was torn up on the inside and the only thing that was keeping me sane was I begging God to please take the pain away. I had no father to protect me and began to feel like the sexual abuse was not important to my mother though I dare not voice that to her as I was taught to respect my elders and my parents no matter what. Besides, I wasn't allowed to speak about it. As I look back, I believe the holy spirit was regulating my mind as there were times I felt like I wanted to die but something would not allow me to muster the courage to carry it out - at least not right then. I also had my studies to help me keep my mind off of things as I was an excellent student and school was like being a different world. I was intelligent, talented, and I knew it. It was something for me to be proud of and gave me a little ambition to be something great.

CHAPTER 2, SELF REFLECTION

Sometimes we have things happen to us in our childhood or adulthood that we never get a chance to address and obtain the necessary help needed to ensure healthy mental, emotional, physical and spiritual development. When this happens, it creates a sense of overwhelming hopelessness and can cause a fear that paralyzes our need to reach out for help, thus creating the perfect sabotage for healing and future relationships. Never allow anyone or anything to separate you from your faith in God, as he will always be the one constant in your life no matter the circumstance.

1.   Is there anything in your childhood or adulthood you can recall that

you think contributes to your fear of reaching out for help or trusting others?

_____

_____

_____

2.   Were you able to obtain the necessary help and support for what you experienced? Why or why not?

_____

_____

_____

Study Scriptures
Matthew 7:8
Proverbs 11:14
Proverbs 28:26
Romans 8:37-39

Chapter 3
INVITING DEMONS IN

Luke 10:19 – *"Behold, I have given you authority to tread on serpents and scorpions, and over all the power of the enemy, and nothing shall hurt you." (ESV)*

My mother had been with the Nation of Islam for a couple of years now. My grandfather passed when I was 13-years-old. I lost my "Daddy." I loved him so much and he would do anything for me. Now one of the people I trusted was gone and I was hurt even more. I still spent a lot of time with my grandmother to keep her company. She was and still is my very best friend.

My mother was the type of woman that wasn't afraid to speak up for herself and she always fought back when my father put his hands on her, but then all of that changed one day. She met a man in the Nation of Islam and little did I know he entered our lives with an evil agenda.

He seemed to be okay at first, but then my sisters and I noticed things about him that we didn't like. He was okay as a conversation buddy, but we didn't want him to be anything more. He had recently been released from prison when my mother met him and we later found out he had been in and out of the system for a while. He acted like he was the biggest man that ever walked the earth. He was disrespectful, had control issues, and had violent tendencies. My mother asked my sisters and I what we thought about him and we gave an honest answer, but she did not listen.

He was mean and nasty to my sisters and I once he began dating my mother. He would curse at my sisters and I and threaten to hit us. My mother would just sit back, watch and say nothing. I noticed that something in my mother had changed drastically. It was like she was almost scared to say something to him. I did my best to protect my sisters and make sure nothing happened to them. I was the very outspoken child and being that my anger and hurt was starting to consume me, it surfaced every now and again since it was never being addressed. From that moment on, I disliked him. He became more disrespectful as time went on and showed more aggression and anger, but now it was just geared towards one of my sisters and I.

I noticed him getting close to my youngest sister and something was telling me that it wasn't genuine. I did my best to try and keep the peace but would definitely speak my mind when necessary. Things became worse and I would try and tell family and other people in the mosque mama attended that things were not right at home but nobody would listen so I began running away from home and even talked my sisters into running away with me once. We ended up at a cousin's house, who then took us right back home. This frustrated me to no end.

I was crying out for help and nobody would help me. I was fatherless, had lost the only earthly father I knew, forced to participate in a faith I did not believe in, was molested, ignored by my mother, and now living with an evil individual. Sooner than later, the demon's agenda would be revealed.

THE SECOND STAB WOUND

I was taught to be a good respectful girl for the most part. I was not a "problem child," if you will. I was a good student in school. I participated in after school programs from elementary through freshman year. I was on the track team, in several choirs and student council. I was on a step team in school too. I got straight A's and was an honor roll student until I became a sophomore in school. I was still a good student, but I got a few B's and C's from time to time as life became more of a burden to bear and my studies suffered a little because of it. As I stated before, school was an escape for me so I participated in everything that interested me.

My mother would let me spend the night with one of my older cousins (who we will call Nancy). Nancy was 20-years-old. She and I were very close. I would talk to Nancy about almost everything. I trusted her and I loved her like a big sister. She always looked out for me when I was with her if I needed her help. My aunt, Nancy's mother, lived with her. I spent part of one summer with my cousin Nancy when I was about 14-years-old because things had been getting worse at home. My mother and I still didn't have a relationship and we didn't talk much.

There was a boy who lived in the same apartment community as my cousin Nancy whom I knew from school. He was a senior in high school. I was going to be a sophomore after the summer was over. He was 19-years-old. I was going to be 15 in a few weeks.

Monroe wasn't a very cute guy but he was okay looking. He approached me and we began to talk on the phone. Even though he wasn't that cute, he seemed like a nice guy so we started to date. The only people that knew we were dating were Nancy and my Aunt.

He used to talk about his mom and his little sister all the time but I hadn't met them yet. He talked highly about his mother and sister so I thought he had the utmost respect for females. One afternoon, he asked if I would come over to his apartment to meet his mother and his sister. I was a little skeptical at first because I had never done anything like that before. We had only been dating for about 4 weeks. I went with him across the parking lot into the apartment. His mother and sister were home. He introduced us. His mother seemed like a very nice lady and his little sister was so cute and sweet. She was about 7. We all talked for a while, then his mother and sister had somewhere to go. I went to follow his mother and sister out the door and head back to my cousin's apartment. He stopped me and asked me to stay for a minute while he got something. I was a little scared but I stayed. I sat in the chair in the living room.

He came back into the living room and I stood up. I told him that my cousin was getting ready to leave in a little bit. We had somewhere to go. He asked me for a kiss. I said ok. I gave him a kiss. He started to wrap his arms around me and I began to get scared. I stopped and told him that I needed to get back across the parking lot. I just kept thinking about the man who had previously violated me and I didn't like to be touched much. He gently grabbed my arm and asked me to stay for just a little bit. I told him no. I didn't want my aunt and my cousin to come looking for me. I started toward the door and He pulled me by my arm a little firmer this time. Again, I thought about the stranger and what happened to me when I was 11-years-old.

I don't think he meant to try and force me, but he was not understanding me when I kept telling him no. That frightened me. He told me he was not going to let me leave until I came into his room. He said he wanted to show me his room. I was not stupid and I knew what that meant. It was just I all by myself in that apartment with him and I didn't have anyone to run to or wake up this time. So I sat down on the bed and I was shaking a little. I tried not to show that I was scared. I figured I would go along with whatever he said and the sooner I did what he asked, the sooner I could leave. He touched my shoulder and felt that I was shaking and told me to relax. "I'm not going to hurt you," he said. "I promise I'll be gentle," he said. I told him that I was a virgin and I did not want to do this. He told me to just relax in a firm tone. I began to cry but tried to suck it up so that he would not see.

I mean I was 14 and he was 19; he was much older than me and I was under age and I was not ready to do this. I had gotten myself into a situation that I did not know how to get out of. I didn't know what would happen if I continued to refuse and I didn't want to find out. I didn't want to make him angry. So I pretended to be okay and I closed my eyes and told myself to be strong. I couldn't stop shaking though. He told me to lay back. He began to remove my pants and my underwear. I placed my hands over my eyes. He got on top of me and he began to have sex with me. I kept my hands over my eyes. I was quiet. I kept thinking about how bad it was hurting. It didn't feel good at all. With my hands still over my eyes, I said, "Please stop, it hurts." He told me to just relax and it only hurt because I was a virgin. He really thought he was doing something, but he was hurting me. I kept my hands over my eyes. He said, "What's my name?" I didn't say anything. He asked me again. It seemed like this went on for a very long time but it only lasted about five minutes. When he was done a tear fell from my eye. He got up. I was silent. I got up, put my underwear and pants back on and left.

I walked in the door and Nancy asked, "Where were you?" I told her where I was and what happened. I didn't tell her that I told him no several times before he had sex with me. I didn't tell her that I tried to leave. I didn't think she or anyone else would believe me because of what happened the first time. I thought people would say it was my fault. I knew if I told the truth, he would just deny it. I just let her believe that it was completely consensual. I didn't tell her that I was scared. We stopped dating after that. We didn't talk to each other anymore after that. My cousin had made jokes about it later on and I just laughed it off.

A couple of days later, my mother came over to my cousin's house. She picked me up and took me for ice cream. I knew something was wrong because we had not done anything like that in a long while, as we were not on good terms. My mother told me that she knew I had sex. I didn't know that she knew. I figured my cousin or my aunt told her. She asked me if I wanted to press charges. She did not know that I had refused him and he did it any way. She only knew what I told my cousin. The fact that he was 19 though made it statutory rape. I thought about it for a minute and I was confused. How could she ask me if I wanted to press charges but had been totally disregarding what happened to me previously and allowing a stranger to come into our house and cause hell? I wanted to tell her the whole truth but I was afraid. I kept it to myself. I thought about what might happen if he did go to jail. Would he be angry and try to hurt me? I told her that I didn't want to press charges. She told me that he had no business being with a 14-year-old. She asked me if I was sure. I said yes. I told her that I didn't want to get anyone in trouble. We never discussed it again.

FINISHING ME OFF

I was now 15-years-old. I started in an environment filled with domestic violence, drugs, and alcohol. I had been without a father. I lost the only real father I knew, forced to conform to Islam, had been molested, raped and living in a house of hell with constant arguing and fighting. I knew my mother loved me and I felt like she had done her best to raise me as a single parent, but somewhere along the way I think she got tired of being alone and just settled for the first man that came along instead of waiting for who she deserved. I began to feel overwhelmed and less important as my mother began to be consumed by her man.

Though God had blessed me with many gifts, talents, I wore nice clothes, and was neatly groomed, deep down on the inside I felt ugly and dirty. I had low self- esteem but I did a good job covering it up. I was very self - conscience. I got many compliments from many boys and mother's friends and so forth but I still felt ugly on the inside. I felt like everybody could see my secrets. I became a very moody person. One minute I would be fine and then I could have an attitude the next for no reason at all. I began to think that nobody cared about me. As a teenager, I just assumed that my mother and those close to me was supposed to already know how I felt. I felt like I was never good enough and everything I did was never good enough for my mother. I felt like she just started to dislike me. She stopped telling me that she loved me. She got so wrapped up in this man that most of their arguments were about me. I always went head-to-head with him. I was constantly voicing my feelings about him to my mother, but she wasn't trying to hear me. She would make me so angry. How could she not see him for what he was?

I began to have suicidal thoughts. Satan really had me then. His plot to murder my mind, body, and spirit was unfolding beautifully for him. He was winning and I was losing. He was successfully destroying me. My heart and spirit was already broken and now he had my mind, that's all he needed to finish me off.

I thought that if I were gone, no one would miss me except perhaps my grandmother. Still 15-years-old, I tried to commit suicide 3 times. Nobody knew except my best friend at the time. We were best friends my freshman and sophomore year of high school. She would pick me up all the time and drop me off. I would spend nights with her and her sister at their mom's house.

One night my mother was gone. She had some type of energy or weight loss pills along with some other prescription drugs in her dresser drawer. I took one of the bottles out and took out some pills. I took them into the bathroom with a cup and began to take one pill after the other. One of my sisters came into the restroom, startling me and I dropped the pills in the sink. I only got to take 2 of them. As I look back, I realize that God always stepped in. He was still present, but I just didn't know how to reconnect. This was my first attempt at suicide – but God!

My mother could always tell when we had been in her things. She asked who was meddling in her drawer and we all denied it. I didn't want her to find out about what I was trying to do. I didn't plan on leaving a note. I just wanted it all to end.

A week later, I went into the kitchen and grabbed a cutting knife. It looked like it would be sharp enough. I took it into the bathroom and closed the door. I put the blade to my abdomen. I began to push it into my abdomen but it wouldn't pierce my skin. I tried jabbing it quickly into my abdomen but it still wouldn't pierce my skin. I managed to cut myself a few times and make some small bruises, but that was it. This was my second suicide attempt – but God!

I continued to grow more and more angry and depressed deep down inside. I began to act out in ways that I never thought I would. I became sexually active on my own this time. I had already had a few boyfriends. I was a beautiful girl on the outside. I dated a lot of boys. I was popular in school. I was never a whore just sleeping with any and every one, but I did begin to have sex with some of the boys I dated. I didn't think enough of myself to respect myself, I guess because I had already been violated and nobody took the time to get me some help to get over it or to let me know that it wasn't my fault. I never turned to drugs or alcohol though. I saw what it was doing to my father and to my relatives on my father's side. I began to hear, "nobody cares about you, loves you, or wants you and nobody ever will." That is what the enemy began telling me and I would constantly re-live everything as to confirm those statements in my head.

I began to contemplate on how to kill myself in a manner that it could not be prevented and would not be very painful, messy, or cause me to struggle. One night I was waiting on my friend to come pick me up. When she called and told me that she was on her way, I made one last attempt to kill myself so that by the time I was dead, I would not be at home. I can't remember where my mother was or what she was doing. I took some Mean Green cleaner from the cabinet and poured it into a glass about half full. I mixed it with just a teaspoon of milk so that it would be easier to swallow. I was in the bathroom once again. I guess I liked going into the bathroom because it was the most private room in the house. I drank it very fast. I didn't feel anything at first. My friend had arrived and I left. I began to sweat and feel like my insides were on fire. As she was driving, she looked over at me. I was moaning. She asked me what was wrong. I told her nothing was wrong and that I would be alright. I was hunched over in my seat. She raised her voice and demanded that I tell her what was wrong with me. I told her that I wanted to die and that I drank some house cleaner. Her eyes got so big. She couldn't believe it. She asked me why I would do such a thing. I told her she wouldn't understand. She told me that she was taking me to the hospital. I begged her not to. She said that she was going to tell her mother what I had done and she would know what to do. We pulled up in front of her mother's apartment. We entered the apartment and I immediately lay on the floor in a ball. My insides felt like they were going to fall right out between my legs. Her mom asked what was wrong. She told her what I had done. Her mom told me that she was going to call my mother and tell her what I did and that she was going to take me to a hospital. It had been bout an hour and a half since I drank the cleaner and I thought to myself, "What is taking so long?" I begged her not to call my mother and not to take me to the hospital. She gave me an ultimatum. Either I let her call my mother and take me to a hospital or I could drink a lot of water to flush the cleaner out of my system and eat something. She wasn't going to have a teenager end up dead in her house on her watch. So I agreed to drink the water and eat the food and she didn't call my mother. I began to cry. My friend asked me why I wanted to kill myself. I told her about the molestation and rape and the problems at home and I just couldn't take it. She was crying and hugging me and telling me that it was going to be okay and that she was there for me if I needed her. I appreciated her for that but I longed for that bond with my mother. My father had already abandoned me. In my mind, I asked God why He wouldn't just let me die. Once again, I made a 3rd attempt, but God! I didn't know it then, but He was there the whole time.

BARREN DIAGNOSIS

I started going through puberty at the age of 10-years-old. At the age of about 13-years-old, I began having very bad pain with my menstrual cycle. I just thought that the older females got, the worse our cramps got. By the time I was 15-years-old, the pain was almost unbearable. I let the pain fester for two whole years. I finally told my mother how bad my pain was during my cycle. She took me to the family doctor at IU hospital. She discovered that I had an extremely severe case of endometriosis. My mother and I hadn't heard of endometriosis. The doctor explained the details, the symptoms, how severe it could be, treatment, and informed us there was no cure. She told us that it could be extremely painful. She suggested that my mother allow me to get a hysterectomy after finding out how extreme my case was.

I had let my symptoms go so long that a hysterectomy was her best solution. My mother wasn't going to allow me to get a hysterectomy without a second opinion. She wanted me to be able to have children and I wanted children. The doctor referred me to a specialist at Riley hospital for children so that my mother could get a second opinion.

After we left the doctor's office, my mother and I went home and got on the Internet to do more research about endometriosis. We found out that it could spread to different parts of the body, if not treated, and it could cause severe pain and even contribute to ovarian cancer. We also found out that it can decrease your chances of having children. In severe cases such as mine, hysterectomy was the final decision. In some cases, women who have children usually don't have the condition anymore. Childbirth seemed to be the only possible cure. There were a very low percentage of patients that experienced symptoms of the condition after having children.

A specialist suggested I try two other options first. She explained a hormonal and surgical treatment. Neither would cure it but they would help slow down the growth. My mother went with the hormonal treatment. As a result, the doctor prescribed birth control pills to slow the growth. I had to take one pill every day and skip the last week and start a new pack in order to keep me from having a cycle. That was the only treatment available besides having a laparoscopy to remove most of the growth. The doctor said, if I were lucky enough to get pregnant, I would have a very difficult pregnancy. I tried to take my life 3 times and now there was a very high chance I was barren. I was beginning to feel as though I could not catch a break to save my life. I thought to myself, "No man is going to love me or marry me because I cannot have children, and even if I did, there is no guarantee I could carry a baby to full term." I began begging God to rescue me, but He didn't seem to show up. That's what I thought at the time, but with maturity came understanding. Much later I learned that He had been there the whole time.

CHAPTER 3, SELF REFLECTION

Sometimes in life we experience things that seem unbearable and when we feel like we are alone or like God is not stepping in fast enough, the enemy begins using that to trick us into believing that God is not present. He may be taunting you by asking, "Where is your God now?" Never forget; not everything you experience is just for you, but may be used as a future testimony to help someone else. Someone had to die to save us and Jesus wasn't guilty of anything. As a child or adult, you may not have been guilty, but He still allowed it. Learn to seek Him in everything and trust His process even when you don't understand it. He may not have caused it, but He allowed it for a reason. Looking back now, I realize it had to happen to prepare me for this appointed time and assignment. When you cannot hear or see God, draw nearer so that you can see through the debris and hear through the noise. When He is silent, know He is busy making a way. Delay is not denial. When it seems He has let go of your hand, it is during those times He is carrying you. He will never put more on you than you can bear. Don't choose to make a permanent decision based on a temporary situation. The trouble won't last forever.

1.   What has or is happening that you feel is worth taking your life over?

---

2.   What are some things you can do that you have never tried to help you draw closer to God and draw strength from Him to endure? Prayer? Fasting? Studying the word? Taking advantage of the help He sends your way?

Study Scriptures
1 Corinthians 10:13
Matthew 24:13
Psalm 34:18
Psalm 147:3
James 4:8

Chapter 4
TWO SHOTS TO THE BACK

Psalm 27:10- *"When my father and my mother forsake me, Then Jehovah will take me up."(ASV)*

Satan couldn't finish me off by means of suicide so the enemy began devising a new plan. I was crawling through life now; I was battling my own thoughts, fears, hurt, pain, anger, abuse and loneliness. I was severely injured and it was like I was laying in the back of a dark alley waiting for someone to walk by and notice I was in need of emergency help; barely able to move.

I continued to argue and express my extreme dislike for my mother's boyfriend. Things only got worse between she and I. He would complain to my mother a lot which would make them argue as well. He was the type of guy who tried to intimidate by talking crazy (making meaningless comments), using profanity, and threatening. If I didn't know anything else about myself, I knew I was a fighter, protector and still found the strength to keep going – even if I was barely holding. I loved my sisters and my mother even though I had been feeling like she didn't love me back at this point. He knew that I was the one that wasn't afraid of him, would stand up against his actions and words towards my sisters and my mother and he didn't like the fact that I would speak my mind about it.

One day my mother packed some things into a black trash bag for one of my sisters and I. She told us to get in the car and neither one of us knew where we were going. We pulled up at the Children's Bureau. The Children's Bureau was a safe place for children and at that time they had a shelter like facility for the children for parents to leave their children. As we sat in the parking lot, my mother told me that I was coming between her and her boy-

43

friend. I was in disbelief; utter shock! I looked at her like she had lost her mind. My mother walked us into the building and we sat down. There was a lady waiting for us, as if she knew we were coming. We looked in our bag and our toothbrushes and clothes were in the bag. My sister and I looked at each other and started crying. I looked at my mother with a very hard look. I was pissed off! Though I was hurt, anger seemed to take over.

My mother left us there and didn't say a word. The lady asked us if we knew why we were there. We told her no. She told us that our mother told her we were very rebellious and she couldn't control us anymore. Now, I didn't understand why my sister was there with me. She didn't like my mother's boyfriend, but she didn't express it as strongly as I did. I told the lady that was a lie. She began explaining what the rules were. We couldn't contact anyone period. Nobody knew where we were but my mother. We couldn't leave at anytime. They had a set time for breakfast, lunch, snack, dinner and bed. It felt like I was in a juvenile detention facility or something similar.

The lady escorted us to a room. On our way to the room, we saw many children and some had been there for a while. We had to speak with a counselor. She told us everything our mother told her and we couldn't believe it. It was just one lie after another. I began telling the counselor what was really going on at home, but she didn't believe me. Nobody would listen. I began thinking about the family members we reached out to, our so-called "friends," and even a few people at the mosque that we reached out to. They refused to believe us. My mother put up a damn good front. I became livid at this point. I could not understand why everyone was turning a blind eye to everything that mattered to me. I began to completely ignore all of the hurt and pain and just became consumed with anger, premeditating revenge. After everything that happened, all the hurt and pain, I was carrying as child. My mother had the audacity to not only ignore how life's circumstances were destroying me, but to get rid of me because her boyfriend. I felt as though she was completely mentally disturbed, at that point in life. There seemed to be no other explanation I could wrap my mind around.

Later that evening or perhaps the next day, I can't recall the exactly, but my mother came back. She came to pick us up. She didn't come on her own. She brought her boyfriend and my little sister. I asked my litter sister what happened, she told me that she asked Mama where we were and begged her to go back to get us. I don't know how true that is, but that is what she told to me years ago.

After returning home, I guess my mother thought her stunt of abandoning me would make me stop verbalizing my dislike for her boyfriend. She didn't realize I had already felt abandoned at the age of 11 when she showed no real concern for the sexual abuse I had just experienced and everything else that took place thereafter. She had not anticipated me voicing my concern even more about the hell in our house created by the demon-possessed man she invited in.

I voiced my opinion to my mother that what she did to my sister and I wasn't right. Her boyfriend jumped into the conversation and it grew into a very heated argument between the three of us. She told me to leave. She told me to get out. I felt like she was choosing a man over her own children.

I stormed up to my room and packed all of my clothes into a huge shopping bag. The next morning, my friend picked me up for school. My mother had slipped a letter in my bag. I can't remember exactly what it said because it was so long ago, but I do remember her explaining why she told me to leave. She told me that I was coming in between her and her boyfriend by being rebellious and disrespectful.

I went out to my friend's car with my bag of clothes. She asked me what I was doing with all of my stuff. I told her that my mother and I got into an argument about her boyfriend and her dropping me off at the Children's Bureau and she told me to get out. I told my friend that I didn't have anywhere to go, but I would try to find somewhere to go by the end of the school day so she could drop me off. My grandmother did not even believe me. My mother had convinced everyone we had this perfect life behind closed doors because that is how she portrayed it out in the open. I didn't believe my mother was a bad or evil person, I just thought perhaps she was experiencing a severe undiagnosed mental disorder and some suppressed issues of her own that clouded her judgement and ability to continue being a mother to me. Unfortunately, I suffered because of it.

I had a boyfriend and I told him after school what happened between my mother and I. I told him that I had nowhere to go and needed to find a safe place to sleep for the night even if it was outside. He told his mom and she let me stay with them for the night.

I remember my cousin Nancy reaching out to me at my boyfriend's house. She asked me what happened and I explained the situation to her. I told her I tried telling our grandmother what happened but my mother had everybody thinking I was just being a rebellious child and didn't want to listen. I knew wrong from right and I knew what was happening wasn't right. I had never been an out of control child or anything of the sort, but I did challenge my mother's decisions as a child. My current emotional and mental state was due to neglect and trying to cope with everything that happened to me. Nancy told me that I could come live with her. The next day, my boyfriend took me to my cousin's house.

Looking back now, I realize God was still there. He provided a way of escape even though I did not identify it as such at that time. My sight was clouded by hurt, pain, anger, resentment and bitterness. Satan was running roughshod and having his way.

DISPATCHED ANGELS

I was 15-years-old, a couple months shy of turning 16, and I felt like the weight of the world was on my shoulders. I had things happen to me that I couldn't discuss with anyone. My relationship with my mother was down the drain. I was missing my sisters. I wanted everything to just be a bad dream.

Living with Nancy and my aunt was a breath of fresh air. I looked up to my cousin, as she was a very young single mother trying to make something more of herself. The next day, Nancy called my mother to tell her where I staying. I never heard from my mother after that anymore, unless Nancy or I called her. She never called to see if I needed anything or to check and see if I was doing well. She didn't offer Nancy anything to help take care of me. I continued feeling angry, disappointed, and sad. I couldn't believe I was being kicked to the curb and treated like an outcast for a man who had some very disturbing tendencies and a need for violence. Unfortunately, as a child, my opinions and thoughts didn't matter to the people I needed most.

Nancy began taking me to school and making sure I got home safely. I decided to get a job. I didn't feel like it was her responsibility to take care of me. She was young and had a baby herself that she was taking care of. I bought my own clothes, shoes, and school supplies, with Nancy's help of course. If I didn't have enough, she would always help me out or just buy me things just because she wanted to. I appreciated and loved her for that. I had no sense of real responsibilities, like bills, at the time. She had expressed to me one day that I never offered her a little money on the bills. I understood. I tried giving her money from time to time when I got paid, if I thought she needed it. She always made sure I ate and she kept a roof over my head. She encouraged me and supported me. She did her very best to make me feel loved and like I had someone to talk to. Had she not taken me in, I think I may have attempted suicide one last time and succeeded.

Nancy knew it had been a very long time since I attended church. She started taking me to services with her and I began to feel better. I immediately joined her church and re-committed my life to Christ. I began singing again and being a part of the youth groups. I had so much fun and enjoyed being in the house of the Lord. I was reconnected to my lifeline.

I was in critical condition, but life became worth living even though the infection growing on the inside could slightly be seen on the outside. The stab wounds, punches, and shots had not received the proper care so there was major internal bleeding. My cousin and aunt became my oxygen, IV, and life support to help stabilize me.

DEFYING THE ODDS

I was now16-years-old and a junior in high school when my mother married her boyfriend. Unfortunately, the reality of what I went through and what my sisters were still going through was finally being brought to the light for all to see.

Since reconnecting with God and having a support system, I began focusing more on school again. I started pursuing my Alterations and Tailoring certification while I was in high school. I had so many talents. I was fortunate to be able to attend a high school that had its own vocational school on the grounds. I couldn't take Cosmetology and Alterations and Tailoring because I had to get my general credits in order to graduate. So, I decided to take Alterations and Tailoring and figured Indianapolis had a lot of Cosmetology schools I could attend after graduation. I wanted to own my own business. I began to dream again. I was coping through everything the devil had thrown at me, but still had not been delivered and healed. I was determined to defy all odds. I had not heard from my mother, although school was going great.

I was doing well with everything, and then my endometriosis started getting worse. The treatment stopped working. My pain was so intense that I was in tears. I began missing school and then I was paralyzed with pain for three days straight. I didn't move at all except to eat and use the restroom. My aunt finally called my mom on the third day and told her that I had been in severe pain and laying the same spot for three days. My mother came and she helped me get dressed and she took me to the emergency room. My body had become immune to the treatment. I was scheduled to have a laparoscopy to remove the endometriosis.

After surgery, I had to go back to my mother's house so that she could do the necessary things to take care of the wound. I didn't expect my cousin to take on such a huge responsibility. I was down for about a week and a half and my mother helped me do just about everything. As soon as I was well enough, I went back to my cousin's house because I really did not want be there, but I had no choice. I felt like she did it out of obligation because she was my mother, perhaps it was the right things for her to do. However, she had not apologized nor had she called to check on me at any time to see if I was okay. Showing up in cases of emergency only would soon become a consistent behavior.

I made a full recovery and went back to school. I missed quite a bit which put me behind and I struggled to catch up, but I was determined to do so. I was put back on the treatment for the endometriosis and it still bothered me from time to time through the rest of junior year and some of senior year, but I was determined to graduate from high school and on time, as I was an excellent student.

One day my mother showed up to pick me up from school to take me to work. I knew instantly that something wasn't quite right considering we were not communicating. I couldn't help feeling that her husband had done something to one of my sisters or someone was dead. I asked her what she was doing there and looked at her with a puzzling yet fearful expression on my face. As she began to drive, she looked at me and confirmed my fear about her husband. My mouth hit the floor! My sisters were in danger and then she did the unthinkable – she blamed his behavior on one of her children. I couldn't believe what I was hearing. Tears began to roll down my face and I became infuriated. I asked her was she going to divorce him. She said, "I don't know." I said, "What!" "What do you mean you don't know?" I knew for a fact at that moment that my mother was not the same woman I knew in my childhood. She made mistakes just like all parents do, but she did her best and then one day she just stopped trying. It seemed like she didn't care whatsoever anymore. It was as if the evil spirits in her husband had now consumed her too. This just made everything I had been trying so hard to suppress and cope with resurface and now resentment began turning into hate.

GAINING SOME CONSCIOUSNESS

I knew my cousin loved me but I was still feeling so empty and even more so now. I was looking for something to fill the void and I didn't know where to turn or how to get it. I reconnected with my godmother who had been in the Navy. I would see her on and off throughout my childhood, but she was back home to stay. I began talking to her and telling her about everything that went on and how I was feeling. She told me that what I was looking for could only be found in God. She said, I have to forgive my mother in order to be able to move forward and be healed, instead of just harboring everything trying to cope. She said I would end up losing my mind if I didn't forgive.

I continued attending church and found that singing or listening to music made me feel something I couldn't explain. It was like I began to feel close to something, but I didn't know what. I began putting all of my hurt, pain, anger, frustration, hate and brokenness onto paper. I wrote a letter to my mother and shared everything I had been holding in and then ended it with forgiveness. I knew I would never get an apology as my godmother told me not to base my forgiveness on whether or not she would admit fault or apologize. What I needed would come from God after I unhardened my heart. I mailed the letter and from that moment on, I began the journey of regaining full consciousness and getting my life back.

HIDING A DEADLY INFECTION

This particular day would prove to be the most terrifying than any other day. Upon finishing my day at school, my best friend at the time dropped me off at work. My cousin was a correctional officer at the time and was supposed to pick me up from work before her shift on this day. I will never forget this day as it is permanently seared into my memory.

I finished my shift at work and waited outside for my cousin to pick me up. I was wearing a black skirt with knee high slits up the sides, a grey and black casual button up shirt with my work shirt thrown over my shoulder and black casual rubber sole shoes. My hair was freshly styled and it was warm outside. My shift ended at 10:00 p.m. and about 10 minutes had passed. The sky and the streets grew darker and the air began to feel muggy. I went back inside to call my cousin to see if she had forgotten to pick me up. No one answered. I got the feeling she forgot about me. I was 16-years-old and though a teenager, I was scared to walk home in the dark when the walk would last an hour at minimum. I thought to myself I didn't have a choice. I needed to get home. So, I began to walk at a quick pace.

The streets were dark and I had a long journey ahead of me. After walking about 25 to 30 minutes, rain began to drizzle and I did not have an umbrella or jacket. I used my work shirt to cover my head. A few minutes later, as I was approaching the entrance of an apartment complex, getting ready to pass it, a stranger in a green Ford four-door SUV approached. It was a man with three young female passengers. He asked if I needed a ride home. I remembered being taught to never talk to strangers or ride with strangers. I declined and tried to keep walking. He pulled up beside me and told me it was too late for me to be walking by myself and asked how old I was. I responded. He began telling me that the passengers were his daughters and they were on their way home, as he needed to get them in the bed, but would not mind giving me a ride home. One of the passengers looked to be about the same age as me, and the others were a few years younger. Only two of the girls were awake. I felt a little scared, but it was very dark, raining, and it would take me *forever* to get home. I accepted and got into the truck.

He began introducing me to the girls and asked my name and then told me I was a pretty young lady. I said thank you and he asked me where I lived. I told him where I lived and he said he knew exactly where it was and would get me home after he dropped his girls off at the apartment to get them in the bed. They lived in the apartments I had just been passing. I said okay.

He parked and they began to get out of the truck. I told him that I would wait outside in the truck. He said he would be a few minutes because he had to get his girls situated and asked me to come in. I was hesitant, but went in anyway. I don't know what was going through my head. I guess the fact he had daughters made me believe he wasn't going to try anything with me. As we walked in, he locked the door behind us and that frightened me. "Why would he be locking the door if we are going to head back out in a couple of minutes," is what I thought to myself. I sat down on the couch as he walked the girls to their rooms for bed. The apartment was very quiet and dark. He walked back into the living room and stood in front of me. I stood up and asked if we could leave. I told him my aunt would be very worried if I didn't show up soon. It was about 11:00 pm by then. He said before we left, he wanted to show me something. I became afraid. I knew something was not right and thought to myself it was going to happen to me again, only this time I was going to die afterwards. I contemplated dashing around him to the door, but I was scared he would catch me. I didn't know what would happen if I screamed, so I just begged him to please let me go home. He told me to calm down and grabbed my hand started towards the back of the apartment. I began praying asking God "don't let me die." I was being held against my will and tried to show no fear, but I was losing that battle quickly.

He was a slim man, average height, low fade, goatee, and chocolate brown skin tone. He smelled of a slight must and was trying to come across as a nice guy, but what he planned on doing to me was going to be anything but nice. He took me into a room where there was a black canopy bed. He closed the door and locked it behind us. I began to cry and told him I really needed to get home. He told me to relax and that I would be able to leave in a few minutes. He told me to lie down on the bed. I couldn't stop crying. I thought that if I just hurried up and did what he said, I would live and still be able to go home. I knew it was getting ready to happen to me again and I couldn't understand why me. He began to undress and I just lay there fully dressed with my eyes closed as tears ran down my face. He lay down next to me and began asking me questions about myself and where I was from while using his hands to unbutton my shirt and fondle me. I asked him to stop and to please let me go. He got on top of me and began undressing me and I cried and pleaded with him to stop. I was shaking uncontrollably and he told me to relax. He whispered, "I'm not going to hurt you." I heard that a lot as a child, but I always ended up hurt anyway. It seemed to be a universal term. I felt so low, dirty, and violated. I felt like I was nothing and a coward for not having the courage to fight back, because my fear of dying overpowered my fear of being raped. As he threw my clothes on the floor, still straddling me, he put his penis in my face and made me perform oral sex. I had no idea what I was doing and began to gag while crying and begging him to stop. He stopped and inserted his penis and began to rape me while he had one of his hands around my neck and telling me how beautiful I was. I lay there with a face full of tears blaming myself. It was my fault. Had I not gotten in the truck with a stranger, none of this would be happening to me. The enemy had me believing I deserved it. When he was finished, he told me to put my clothes back on. I begged him to let me go. After that, some of it is a fog. I remember leaving the apartment crying. I don't remember the rest of the walk home, but I know I made it there and my aunt asked me what took me so long and why I was crying. I told her Nancy forgot to pick me up. I dare not say a word about what just happened to me. I just kept thinking about how I was made to believe these things were my fault and I just knew she would be mad at me for getting in the truck. I never spoke a word about it to anyone.

The next day, I was upset and asked my cousin why she didn't come pick me up. She said she forgot. I told her it took me forever to get home. She didn't know it, but I blamed her a little for what happened to me. From that point on, I didn't care much about having sex, even if I was dating the person. I put on a smile for everyone and pretended nothing happened.

CHAPTER 4, SELF REFLECTION

It may seem like you can never catch a break; like it is just one thing after another, but understand that God is still in control. There may be times where we can prevent certain circumstances and when are able to identify those times, be sure to take the necessary precautionary measures. Always remember that God can be any and everything you need Him to be. He can be a mother, a father, a friend, a provider, etc. He may use others to do that, but He is still fulfilling His promise that He would will never leave you nor forsake you. No matter who you feel has abandoned you or violated you, He will be with you until the very end. Remember that it is the enemy's job to make you believe you are less than what God says you are and created you to be, but tune his lies out and don't allow his annoyance to make you follow what it is he wants you to do. TO EVERY INDIVIDUAL THAT HAS EXPERIENCED ABANDONMENT OR ABUSE IN ANY WAY; IT IS NOT YOUR FAULT. God loves you, and so do I.

1.   Is there anything you feel continues to happen to increase the pain, hurt, resentment or bitterness you feel? If so, can it be prevented in any way? Who do you need to forgive?

_____

_____

_____

2.   How will you defy the odds? What steps can you take to show the enemy you believe what and who God says you are?

_____

_____

_____

Study Scriptures
James 4:7
1 Peter 5:8
Ephesians 6:16

Chapter 5

TREATMENT FOR INFECTION

Immediately just graduating from high school, I met the man of my dreams, so I thought. We talked a little and I wasn't interested at first, but eventually we began to date. There wasn't a day that went by that he was not at my cousin's house to see me. He took me out every weekend. He seemed like the perfect gentleman.

About a month and a half later after meeting the young man, I found myself getting into an altercation with my cousin Nancy in front of him about my mother. Nancy told me that she was moving again and I needed to find somewhere to go. I said, "Okay." Out on the porch, he asked if I was okay. I told him "yes," but I needed to figure out where I was going to go. He offered to let me stay with him and his roommate. I told him that I would have to think about it because I didn't know him very well. I didn't want to move in with two young men that I really didn't know, but where else was I going to go? He was only two years older than me. He was 19 and I was 17. I didn't think that he would try and do anything bad to me but of course I felt like I needed to be cautious given my previous experiences. I could be very cold and mean sometimes. I had to look out for me so that nobody else would ever hurt me the way I had been hurt before.

I began to think of other places I could go. I still had my job but I wasn't making enough money to pay for an apartment and I wasn't old enough yet to even apply for one in my name. So I tried to figure out where I was going to go because Nancy was moving in a couple of weeks. I called him the next day and told him that I couldn't find anywhere else to go. I asked him if he made sure that it was ok with his roommate. He said that his roommate was okay with it and he was rarely at home anyway. So I accepted his offer. I moved in that weekend. Shortly after, we officially became a couple. We were living together and we were having premarital sex. Now that I look back, I realize that I had no business calling myself being in a relationship when I had not dealt with the demons I was harboring. I just knew I wanted to love someone and feel loved in return.

We began doing everything together. I was not a very affectionate person as I had been violated too many times and didn't like anyone really touching me. I didn't even like to really hug people either. He understood that and was trying to be patient with me. I began to open up slowly but surely as he assured me I could trust him and that he wouldn't do anything to hurt me. His actions so far, were evidence of his words. We had so much fun. He treated me with the utmost respect and I absolutely adored him.

He asked me if I belonged to a church. I told him "no," but I wouldn't mind finding a church home. I mean I thought he was the perfect guy. He had 2 jobs, his own place, and a nice car, went to church, and was saved. He liked a lot of the same things that I liked and he spent a lot of time with me. He told me often how beautiful I was, he paid attention to me and he comforted me when I was sad about the things that were going on with me.

Shortly after, he took me to meet his parents. When I walked in the door, his mother greeted me with a big smile and a hug. She was a very warm and kind woman. She was also a very godly woman. His father was a very quiet man. He spoke and smiled. His mother said, "You're a pretty little girl." I said, "Thank you." I laughed because she called me a little girl. She asked me many questions about myself. She also asked how her son was treating me. I told her that he was treating me just fine. This would be the beginning of being "adopted" into a close-knit family.

STABILIZATION

I went to church with my boyfriend one Sunday. He was close to the pastor, his wife, and their family. They had claimed him as their son. I couldn't believe my ears when the pastor opened his mouth to preach. I could see instantly that there was something special about this man and that he was very anointed. He really delivered the word of God in a way that you could understand it and he was raw, real, and relevant. He didn't sugar coat a thing. He told it just like it was. I enjoyed myself so much that I continued to go with my boyfriend every Sunday. I could tell that he was a very likable and lovable person because of all the people that had adopted him as a son. He introduced me to several of his friends and his many adopted parents. I felt right at home for the first time in a long time. I felt like I belonged. Everyone was so welcoming. He introduced me to the pastor and his wife. I was headed for recovery and didn't even know it.

The pastor and his wife took a liking to me too. They invited my boyfriend and I over to their house. My boyfriend began to brag about how wonderful and talented I was. I had never heard someone speak so highly of me and it felt a little uncomfortable because of what lie beneath the pretty smile and plethora of gifts and talents. Pastor put me on the spot and asked me when I could sing a solo at church during altar call. I had never done that before. I sang in many places, even churches, but didn't feel I should be singing during altar call, but accepted. Pastor asked me about my life, where I came from and I told him a little bit about my past. He became my spiritual father and counseled me through a lot of the hurt, habits, and hang-ups. I also attended a "Victims to Victory" program that was like spiritual group therapy for those who had been abused or were the abusers. The classes covered everything from generational curses to different forms of abuse to suicidal thoughts.

I was finally getting the help I needed to feel whole again for the first time in a very long time. There would be no more internal bleeding and my wounds would begin to heal properly. The classes and the counseling along with building a relationship with Jesus helped me to gain strength and I was ready to face my demons along with anything else Satan was going to try and throw at me from that point on. I was broken emotionally, mentally, and physically at that time, but my spirit was never broken – only bruised. He couldn't kill me because my spirit refused to die.

PREMATURE REHAB

My boyfriend and I got engaged in 2002. I was 18-years-old and he was 20. He was very good to me. I loved him unconditionally and I believed that he loved me the same. The year and a half we had been together was beautiful and though we had our disagreements, we worked through them. I was still having trouble in certain areas because of my past, but he still wanted to be with me. I was on cloud nine. Little did I know he had some issues of his own that I did not see until it was too late.

He knew about my health condition. My treatment for the endometriosis stopped working again a year later in 2003. It had been a year since the doctor had increased my dose. I was in excruciating pain. Upon visiting the doctor, she explained to me that the only other options I had were to get the hysterectomy or to try and get pregnant. She left my fiancé and I alone to discuss what we wanted to do. I wasn't really ready for children and neither was he, but we both wanted children eventually. Since the hysterectomy was out of the question, we decided to try and get pregnant. The doctor came back into the room and we told her that we wanted to try and get pregnant. She prescribed some kind of pill to help me get pregnant. She explained that I had a minimal chance at getting pregnant, but if I did, my pregnancy would be high risk and very difficult.

Two weeks before the wedding, I found out that I was pregnant. God sure did know how to perform a miracle. I had a rough pregnancy from the beginning. One morning, I woke up and there was blood in the bed. I thought I was having a miscarriage. I rushed to the emergency room. The doctors told us that I wasn't having a miscarriage, but they needed to run tests to see where the blood was coming from. The doctor couldn't tell us what the problem was, she just gave us a few guesses on other reasons why I would be bleeding and told us to come back if it didn't stop or if it got worse. We continued making final arrangements for the wedding. On Saturday, March 22, 2003, we were married. It was one of the happiest days of my life.

Upon returning from the honeymoon, I started having a lot of problems with the pregnancy. I continued to have bleeding on and off and some pressure. I was rushed to the emergency room at 5 months pregnant. The doctors put an oxygen mask on my face and started sticking a baby zapper up the birth canal, but would not tell us what was going on. She wasn't moving. The doctor began to tell me that the baby's heart rate was dangerously low to the point that I might lose the baby. I began to cry. I ended up being admitted for a week and a half due to the baby having a severely low heart rate. The baby had to be monitored around the clock. Upon being released, I was put on bed rest for the last five months of the pregnancy.

While on bed rest, my husband seemed to be working more than usual and began coming home later and later every day of the week. I knew in my gut that something wasn't right, but I didn't say a word.

I gave birth to my first bundle of joy on November 20, 2003. She was the most beautiful gift I had ever seen. When she was born, her heart proved to be perfect. She was absolutely perfect! I couldn't help but say, "Thank you Jesus," because by the time she got here, God reached inside of my womb and fixed the problem with her heart. She was my miracle baby two times over.

SUSTAINING NEW INJURIES

I had been married for nine months now and shortly after giving birth, it was confirmed that my husband's late nights and sudden disrespectful tone with me had everything to do with infidelity. I was heartbroken and I couldn't believe the man I had fallen in love with, whom I trusted after everything I had gone through would turn around and hurt me. A few weeks later, he told me he did not want to be married anymore and was moving out. I knew I had done nothing wrong, at least nothing to deserve this type of treatment. I cooked, cleaned, worked, supported and prayed for him, but above all was faithful. I was beside myself and was so distraught, my blood pressure spiked severely and I passed out. I woke in the hospital with him there and I just began to cry. All I could think about was our daughter and everything I went through to make sure she made it into this world and how much of a miracle she was.

I had a newfound strength and this time, I wasn't going to just sit back and allow another man or anyone else to violate or hurt me on purpose. We argued and went back and forth for a while and then he moved out. It was hard to even get up and out of the bed in the morning for a while. I was so consumed with sadness, loneliness, and anger that I stopped caring, but I couldn't shake the fact I loved him. Eventually, the sorrow took over the anger and I began evaluating myself to see if there was something wrong with me or something I did to make him want to cheat and leave me abruptly. There was that "it's my fault" mentality again. I was still taking responsibility for other people's actions.

We would see each other back and forth and even attended marriage counseling with the pastor, but he continued doing whatever he wanted to do as if he knew I would never leave him. That all changed after he realized the grass wasn't so green on the other side after trying to water it for 3 months. He came back home and promised things would be different. I believed him and forgave him. I didn't believe in divorce as I knew marriage was a very serious covenant and I didn't want my child growing up in a single parent home like I did. I was determined to put in the work necessary to make my marriage work. Every good thing requires maintenance, and true love is consistent no matter what.

CHAPTER 5, SELF REFLECTION

Oftentimes we confuse coping with healing. Coping suggests you have found a way to co-exist with what you still possess but need to release in order to move forward without finding yourself back where you started repeatedly. Healing suggests you have found a way to live through exercising forgiveness and participatory deliverance to rid yourself of the toxic matter that hindered your ability to move forward. Sometimes we feel if we don't seize the opportunity right then, we may lose who has entered our life. We must understand that if God placed them there, then it is for you – and whatever God has for you, is for you. You don't have to worry about losing them if they are God sent. During your healing process, allow God to strengthen your spirit by filling you with His spirit, loving you through who He sent, providing for you through any vessel He sees fit, and supporting you through them as well, while He focuses on healing you everywhere you hurt. He may even use them to save your life as He did in my case. When the time is right, God will release you. They will still be there, if they are meant to be for your lifetime. If not, it means they were there for a season and there will be someone coming behind them meant for more than a season – a lifetime. You too will be worth the wait for them. You cannot fully enjoy what He has for you until you deal with the fear of losing it. Perfect love casts out fear. It is a process. Let Him work.

1.   Have you tried to move on to new things and relationships without allowing yourself the necessary time to heal? Was it for fear of losing what you have gained?

_____

_____

_____

2.   Are you willing to slow down and take your time to make sure you are able to enjoy the fullness of what He has for you? What steps do you need to take to make sure this happens? When will you make the necessary changes?

_____

_____

_____

Study Scriptures
Psalm 147:3
1 Peter 5:7
Philippians 4:6-7
2 Timothy 1:7
1 John 4:18

Chapter 6
BRAIN DAMAGE

Shortly after my husband returned home, I found out that I was pregnant with our second child. Things were okay for a little while. Soon after, I noticed the same old behavior had resurfaced.

A few weeks later, I found out that my husband was still keeping in contact with the young girl he had an affair with, and now she too was pregnant. I was beside myself. I called pastor to get some regulation to my thoughts because they were not pleasant. He insisted that my husband and I see him right away. I got into my car and I cried and yelled and asked God "Why" the whole way to the church. It was as if I'd been traumatized with pain.

The meeting with our pastor didn't go well. My husband made me angrier as he behaved in such a nonchalant manner. I had to do something and the devil had me once again. I was being controlled by my anger, hurt, and the enemy began whispering again, "Told you nobody would ever love you or want you." I felt numb, completely dead on the inside and yet, I still gave everything I had left to my precious baby girl.

I told my husband that even though I didn't believe in abortion, I was thinking about getting one. I was so ashamed and the pain that I was going through was unbearable at that time, so I thought. He told me that he didn't care if he had another girl pregnant at the same time as me and if I went through with an abortion, he would divorce me. He was mean, cruel and nonchalant about the whole situation. I became very angry and sad. I couldn't believe he was acting like he hadn't done anything wrong. After knowing what he had done, he had the audacity and the gall to speak to me like that. I began to cry and at that moment I decided that I would try to get rid of the baby another way. It wasn't that I didn't want the baby entirely; I just didn't want to be pregnant by my husband at the same time that he got his mistress pregnant. I began taking my birth control pills to try and miscarry. I took them for the first trimester and when nothing happened, I gave up. I never told my husband what I had done. I began asking God to help me accept it and I realized that I loved my child more than trying to hide my shame. I was repenting and asking God for forgiveness for what I had just done. God had given me the miracle to have children after the doctors told me I couldn't and I was allowing the enemy's new tactics of trying to break me, make me behave way outside of my character.

As time passed, things had gotten worse between my husband and I. He began cheating with countless women, passed a sexually transmitted disease to me while I was pregnant, and had become very evil toward me. I was no longer allowed to sleep in the same room with him, let alone the bed. I was pregnant with our son who was also a high-risk pregnancy, and I was forced to sleep on the floor or the couch in the living room. I put up with verbal and emotional abuse constantly. We put on a very good front, as I was so ashamed and hurt and didn't want anyone to know what I was going through. I felt so stupid.

I gave birth to a beautiful baby boy on Christmas day of 2004. He looked so perfect, but he was born with a minor complication and I began to cry and remember I tried to abort him during the first trimester. I told my husband what I had done and he told me that the doctor said it was common among baby boys and it wasn't my fault. I still felt responsible. After two weeks, the problem fixed itself and he was even more perfect than the day I laid eyes on him. I began experiencing postpartum depression and tried my best to hold it all together. I was dealing with so much but I kept telling myself, "If nobody else needs or wants me, my children need me."

Our marriage began crumbling as the cheating had reached its peak along with the verbal and emotional abuse. He began staying away from home days at a time. He came and went as he pleased. No matter what I tried to change about me or how sweet I was toward him, it made him treat me worse. I began taking classes at church that gave me peace, comfort, and encouragement while I was going through at home. God gave me the strength to endure and eventually I became silent. I focused on our two children who were one year old and 4 months at the time. I completely ignored my pain and became numb to the mean and nasty words and treatment for a little while. I was losing me. I became wrapped up in a man rather than wrapped in Jesus.

HEART ATTACK

After a while, I felt my mind getting the best of me and I started having suicidal thoughts once again. I began to confide in my husband's mentor's wife. I also began to confide in my children's godmother. My husband didn't like this but I needed to talk to someone so that I could stay in my right mind. They were my only friends at this point in my life that I trusted with information about my marriage and my mental state other than pastor because they kept it confidential.

I began keeping a journal and writing about the events that had taken place on a daily basis as a means of releasing frustration and hurt. I felt myself slipping away slowly but surely. I called pastor and told him that I needed to check into a mental facility because I felt myself reaching a breaking point and I was on the brink of having a nervous breakdown. He asked me why I felt that way. He told me that I didn't need to go to a facility. He told me that I should just pray and ask God to show me what I should do. He prayed for me on the phone and told me to call if I needed anything.

When my husband returned, I told him that I was going to leave and that I was taking the kids and the pictures with me, along with our clothes and their toys. He told me that I wasn't going to leave him. He always used to tell me, *"You ain't going nowhere; you ain't never going to leave me."* He continued to argue with me and told me that he wanted me to be miserable. I just became silent and tried to convince myself to pack our things and wait for him to leave so that I could escape the hell I was living in. I couldn't stop myself from cracking mentally because emotionally I was a wreck but I continued writing in my journal to release as much as I could:

> **JOURNAL ENTRY:** *"Saturday, 6/4/05*
> *This week has really been a down week for me. You know, JR has done nothing but bitch at me and complain about everything. If the tables were turned, I wouldn't act anywhere near as raunchy as he has. He talks to me and treats me with so much disrespect. He's actually threatened me twice this month. Today he said something to the fact that he was going to hit me. It's so emotionally draining to have someone constantly put you down, talk*

down to you, talk about you, and talk to you like you're
nothing in front of other people..."

JOURNAL ENTRY: *"Sunday, 6/5/05*

By this time, I was just full of anger and my eyes began to
fill with tears. I became so overwhelmed with rage that I
started to sit there and watch him sleep. I thought about
suffocating him with a pillow. I could actually see him
gasping for air in my mind. I mean why would he do such
a thing? I turned the TV to the church channel so that I
could get in my right mind before I completely snapped."

RESUSCITAION

A couple of days passed and we had a long talk about our marriage. He told me that he wanted a divorce. I was shocked! He was the one cheating, but he wanted the divorce. I sat and put up with this hell from him for 3 years straight after giving him 5 years of my life and only for him to turn around and divorce me... me! I couldn't believe that my life was falling apart yet again. The only thing I had left was my love for my children. It was happening again. The enemy was winning the battle in my mind and the self-destruction began:

JOURNAL ENTRY: *"Tuesday, 6/7/05*
You are good for nothing and you ain't nothing but a debt
to me. You ain't ever done anything for me or helped me.
The only thing you ever did that was good was give me 2

children. I don't like you and I don't care about you either. I don't want to be with you. You can leave."

JOURANAL ENTRY: *"Wednesday, 6/8/05*
...if he would have stabbed me a few times, it would hurt just the same. ...he said he didn't mean what he said because he just said it out of anger, but then he turned around today and said almost the same thing."

My husband left and I had finally cracked. The devil had won this battle. I had a mental breakdown. I walked to the corner to use the pay phone and I called my husband's mentor and told him to come and get my kids because I was going to kill myself. I didn't want my children left in the home with their dead mother for hours before someone found them. I loved my children dearly and decided they too would be better off without me. My love, compassion, protection, support, loyalty and relentless efforts to withstand the storms with others were never enough – not then and not now. I felt like I never got any reciprocity.

I walked back into the house and began thinking about everything that my husband had said to me; everything that was done to me, and every promise that was broken and began to cry. I knew I would just be better off dead. I thought about hanging myself or getting a knife and slitting my wrists. My children were crying but I ignored them. It was like I was in the room but I had stepped outside of myself. I went to the kitchen to get a knife and I sat in the middle of the floor crying and yelling at God. I put the knife to my left wrist and right before I had the chance to slit my wrist, my husband's mentor came bursting through the door. He saw my children in the playpen crying. He looked at me sitting in the middle of the floor crying and repeating "I can't take it anymore." He kneeled down, took the knife and laid it on the floor and wrapped his arms around me and he kept telling me, "It's going to be alright." It seemed like everything I had been holding in began to flow right out of me through my tears and into his embrace. He told me the ambulance was on its way.

On the way to the hospital, the EMT asked me why I wanted to kill myself and if I was going to harm my children. I told them that I would never harm my children. They had nothing to do with what I was dealing with. I arrived at the hospital and my husband showed up. I didn't even turn in the bed to look at him. Tears just began to roll down my face. He was apologizing and telling me that he didn't mean what he said. I never said a word to him. I was put on suicide watch and had to speak to a psychiatrist. Later, the psychiatrist gave me a number to call to set up an appointment with a therapist to get some ongoing help and I was released.

ROAD TO RECOVERY

A few days went past and my husband had been reading my journal. He confronted me about it and asked me why I felt the way I did. He asked me if I wanted the divorce. I told him no. I told him that I was willing to keep trying but that it wouldn't work if both parties didn't agree and make an effort. He agreed that we would work on it, but things became a whole lot worse instead of better. I almost lost my children and my life. After attending church, I knew that I had to do what was best for me, but more importantly, for my children.

At the end of June 2005, I decided I was going to leave my husband. I made up in mind that I had enough. I was not going to let the enemy trick me any longer or convince me that I wasn't worth God's best. I knew fixing me wasn't going to be easy, but I knew He was the only one that could do it. I didn't tell my husband I was leaving. I decided I would wait until he left for work, then I would take the kids and get out of there. I called my husband's mentor's wife and I explained to her that I wanted to leave but I didn't know where I was going to go. She had arranged for me to stay with her mother. I had never met her mother but I trusted her judgment. Even though I was a little scared having to leave and start completely over with 2 babies, I decided I had to go forward anyway. I was done being my husband's doormat and I was determined to make it.

Divorce was hard, but it was necessary as the infidelity and abuse seemed it was never going to end. Needless to say, God finally had my undivided attention instead of my problems. I had to become everything he intended for me to be and I was determined to obtain everything he had for my babies and I. After everything I had encountered from childhood up until this point, I knew I had some extraordinary blessings and assignments in the future. I also knew the healing process would be long and painful, but necessary.

There is so much more to the story and I would love to share with you my full recovery experience as it has some very practical tips and steps you could apply to your recovery experience on the way to living a life of no limits. Stay tuned for part two; "Rehab," and learn about how my struggle to be obedient and conquer everything along with God using homelessness and a few other things to grab my undivided attention catapulted me into total liberation, success, and prosperity! Don't ever give up on God. He will never give up on you!

You have walked with me through discovering the roots of my behaviors and thought processes that hindered my ability to succeed in life. I hope I have given you some encouragement and a little help in discovering your own. Now, let's prepare to accomplish the hard part; putting in the work to fix it.

As we evaluate our current situations, thought processes and behaviors, we recognize the areas that need immediate attention in order to be able to move forward. We must be willing and honest with ourselves and stop the lies. Lying to everyone about who we are and what we are feeling. In addition, isolation only causes the spread of the deadly infectious disease. The spread of the infection is caused by our refusal to explore and pull up the roots of our current mental, emotional, spiritual and physical state. This negatively influences our behavior, therefore pouring over into our children and communities and ultimately hindering our ability to live free. We must discover all of the roots that caused the cracks in our foundation so that we may begin to rebuild with a firm foundation.

I had to go through the long and painful process of revisiting the roots of my issues, current behaviors and decisions in order to keep me from continually going in circles and not walking in my purpose. As we enter the "REHAB" part of this series, we will discover that this is the area where the enemy will fight you the hardest. You will experience some withdrawals as well as some relapses, but no matter what, don't quit. As I entered REHAB, I fell into a few moments of withdrawal and relapse and experienced more injuries trying to do it all on my own instead of following the steps given to me by the therapist (God). Slipping into explosive and vengeful behaviors, domestic violence, homelessness, and even having an abortion seemed to paint a picture that I was not recovering. Defeat seemed to be my outcome, but brokenness, humility and determination kicked in and victory was soon in sight. Divine intervention and strategically placed help along the way helped me to hear, receive and believe the promises of God for my life. It brought me to where I am today; I am living a life without limits and enjoying the fruits of my labor. Owning your own business, starting an organization, becoming the parent you know you can be, living debt free, developing a right relationship with God, finding your "Ruth" or "Boaz," furthering your education, no matter what your goals are they are more than possible to accomplish. I am living it right now and I should not even be here, but God's grace is sufficient. So, let's go to work, and let me walk you through some practical exercises and rebuilding tips on how to fight the withdrawals and relapses as you begin REHAB and rebuild your life! Come on and go with me.

CHAPTER 6, SELF REFLECTION

Remember that life and death are in the power of the tongue. Be careful about the company you keep and what they speak into your spirit. The words have just as much power to destroy you as actions do. Never allow yourself to be consumed by other human beings, as people are not your God.

Ignoring the root of issues will cause you to function abnormally emotionally, mentally, spiritually, and even physically. It hinders your ability to communicate in a healthy manner as well as build healthy relationships. Always remember who God says you are and use the power He gave you over the enemy. Remember that God will forgive you and cleanse you if you confess your sins and repent. He has the power to re-establish you and restore your joy. Make up in your mind that enough is enough, make the choice to face everything that has found its way inside of you that is not like Him and begin the removal process.

1.   Have you had enough? What company do you keep that needs to be removed? What have they spoken into your spirit?

_____

_____

_____

2.   What do you need to be forgiven for? What counsel will you seek? Spiritual? Therapeutic?

_____

_____

_____

Are you ready for full recovery? Well, join me in the next book in this 3-part series, *Rehab*, so I can encourage you through it.

Study Scriptures
1 Corinthians 15:33
Proverbs 14:7
Proverbs 22:24-25
1 John 1:9

www.ingramcontent.com/pod-product-compliance
Lightning Source LLC
Chambersburg PA
CBHW060142050426
42448CB00010B/2247